CONTENTS

WHISTLING THORN
By Helen Cowcher

ABOUT THE SERIES
INSIDE FRONT COVER

BACKGROUND INFORMATION
3-5

LESSON PLANS
6-20

LET'S LOOK AT THE BOOK COVER	6
THE MAIN EVENTS	7
FINDING OUT MEANINGS OF WORDS FROM THE TEXT	8
GIRAFFE'S POINT OF VIEW	9
ADJECTIVES	10
READING AND WRITING NON-FICTION	11
READING COMPREHENSION	13
GIRAFFE POEMS	14
RETELLING THE STORY	15
USING CONJUNCTIONS	16
COMPOUND WORDS	17
STORY WRITING	18
BOOK REVIEW	20

PHOTOCOPIABLES
20-32

PREDICTING THE STORY FROM THE COVER	21
THE FOUR MAIN EVENTS OF THE STORY	22
MATCHING WORDS AND MEANINGS (1)	23
MATCHING WORDS AND MEANINGS (2)	24
WHAT IS THE GIRAFFE SAYING?	25
COMPREHENSION (1)	26
COMPREHENSION (2)	27
COMPREHENSION (3)	28
CONJUNCTIONS (1)	29
CONJUNCTIONS (2)	30
COMPOUND WORDS	31
HOW THE ROSE GOT ITS THORN	32

SKILLS GRID
INSIDE BACK COVER

CREDITS

Published by Scholastic Ltd,
Villiers House,
Clarendon Avenue,
Leamington Spa,
Warwickshire CV32 5PR
Text © Angela Buckle
© 1998 Scholastic Ltd
1 2 3 4 5 6 7 8 9 0   8 9 0 1 2 3 4 5 6 7

Author Angela Buckle
Series Consultant Fiona Collins
Editor Kate Pearce
Series designer Lynne Joesbury
Designer Clare Brewer
Illustrations Robin Lawrie / Gaye Galsworthy
Cover illustration Helen Cowcher

Designed using Adobe Pagemaker

British Library Cataloguing-in-Publication Data
A catalogue record for this book is available from the British Library.

ISBN 0-590-54709-7

The right of Angela Buckle to be identified as the Author of this Work has been asserted by her in accordance with the Copyright, Designs and Patents Act 1988.

All rights reserved. This book is sold subject to the condition that it shall not, by way of trade or otherwise, be lent, hired out or otherwise circulated without the publisher's prior consent in any form of binding or cover other than that in which it is published and without a similar condition, including this condition, being imposed upon the subsequent purchaser.

No part of this publication may be reproduced, stored in a retrieval system, or transmitted, in any form or by any means, electronic, mechanical, photocopying, recording or otherwise, without the prior permission of the publisher. This book remains copyright, although permission is granted to copy pages 21 to 32 for classroom distribution and use only in the school which has purchased the book and in accordance with the CLA licensing agreement. Photocopying permission is given for purchasers only and not for borrowers of books from any lending service.

BACKGROUND INFORMATION

GENRE

Whistling Thorn is a picture book with an environmental theme set in Africa. The illustrations are bold and colourful, and evocative of the hazy heat of the African plains. While the book is factually accurate in its description of the evolution of the acacia bush, the explanation is told within a story format. The animals in the book, the rhino and the giraffe, do not have individual characteristics – they do not speak or express their feelings – but are used as a means of telling the story. It is a challenging text and theme for Key Stage One.

PLOT SUMMARY

The story describes how, in the grasslands of Africa, the acacia buds were the favourite food of many of the animals. Unlike the rhinos who only ate moderately from the bushes, the giraffes grazed constantly from them and, as a consequence, the bushes began to die out. The acacias grew thorns, which looked like galls, to protect themselves. Attracted by their sweet smell, ants began to inhabit the galls. They made a hole to enter the galls and, when the wind blew across the plains, it 'whistled' through the holes. When the giraffes tried to eat from the acacia bushes, the ants were disturbed and crawled all over the giraffes' muzzles. The ants, rather than the thorns, ended up being the acacias' protectors, as the giraffes moved on when they were stung, thus allowing the bushes to grow fresh leaves.

ABOUT THE AUTHOR

Helen Cowcher is an author and illustrator who lives in South London. She has a particular interest in the natural world and environmental issues. She studied at the Chelsea School of Art and, while there, undertook commissions for black and white botanical drawings – a contrast to the bold and colourful illustrations she uses in her picture books.

Through teaching for one day a week and designing for advertising and packaging, she was able to afford more time for her painting, and also for travelling. A trip to India proved to be life-changing for her and she has included the images and impressions of this visit in subsequent work.

Each of Helen Cowcher's books takes about a year in production – from researching and planning to the final version. Her illustrations are striking and vibrant with colour; she dampens the paper so that more of the water colour she uses soaks in. Her intention is that her pictures are not 'life-like', but capture the nature and spirit of her subjects. Cowcher has learned to be sparing with text – she manages to convey her story with the minimum of text to picture.

SPECIFIC TEACHING OPPORTUNITIES

Please note that there is a Big Book version of *Whistling Thorn* available from Scholastic Ltd which is ideal for use in the Whole-class work session.

Many of the sessions have a photocopiable sheet which accompanies the activity. In some sessions more than one photocopiable sheet is provided. Where indicated these are ability-differentiated; the first photocopiable sheet being for more able children, the second photocopiable being for middle ability children and the third photocopiable being for younger or less able children. Some activities may provide

BACKGROUND INFORMATION

only two photocopiable sheets. On these occasions the first sheet is for the more able children and the second sheet for less able children.

TEXT LEVEL

Whistling Thorn offers many opportunities for text level work. The issues that arise in it, supported by the beautiful illustrations, will encourage children to want to find out more about the animals, Africa and environmental concerns.

The author uses text sparingly to tell the story and it is important, therefore, to establish the key events in the book – the fact that the acacia bushes were being wiped out by the constant grazing; that they grew thorns to protect themselves; that the ants made their homes in the galls, which meant they became 'whistling thorns'; and that the giraffes were finally stopped from eating the bushes because the ants crawled over them when their homes were disturbed.

In order to strengthen children's understanding of the story and its context, it is helpful for them to find out something about the country and the animals. Cowcher's vivid pictures convey a sense of the intense heat of the African plains. With the class explore the ways in which the landscape in the book is different from the environment the children live in. Simple comparisons can be made to contrast these locations. Discussion can also centre around how the book could be written as an information book.

The author has stated that she has made a point of using the minimum of text, and the story is very much a 'bare-bones' structure. Encourage the children to elaborate when they retell it for themselves, using storytelling language and developing appropriate techniques to describe the scenes in more detail. They can also expand the characters' roles by using dialogue. Draw comparisons with other books which have animal characters in which the animals *do* speak or convey their feelings, such as, *Farmer Duck* by Martin Waddell or *Bob the Dog* by Vivian French.

The story can be used as a model for children to write their own stories. It can be used as a 'scaffold' on which to base a story of 'How the rose got its thorn', for example. An aspect or feature of the story can also be used as a starting point for a poem – about the giraffe or the rhino, an environmental issue or descriptive work from Cowcher's illustrations.

Despite the book's simplistic structure, it manages to convey the complex idea of how plants adapt and evolve to survive. The theme of survival is one that can be pursued as a follow-up activity, for example the children can find out how plants and living creatures protect themselves through defences, camouflage and adaptation to the environment in which they live.

SENTENCE LEVEL

The story is written in fairly long sentences that are, for the most part, relieved by commas. Children need to be aware that this is an indication that they should pause before reading on. This is particularly important when they are reading the story aloud. Show the children how the long sentences can be split up into shorter, and sometimes more manageable sentences. Alternatively, the sentences can be joined by using conjunctions.

The story is told in the past tense. This can be used as a vehicle for work on tenses. The children can look for words that end with 'ed' and change the text to the present tense.

The rich language of the text is ideal for teaching aspects of grammar, such as parts of speech. The author's use of many and varied adjectives will provide opportunities for the children to discuss and show their understanding of them, using them in sentences and in work of their own.

BACKGROUND INFORMATION

WORD LEVEL

Whistling Thorn contains a lot of challenging vocabulary for Key Stage One children and much of it will need to be explained. This presents an ideal context for introducing and practising dictionary skills. As a class activity you may like the children to compile a glossary that can accompany the book to help when reading. Other dictionary and thesaurus work can be based on finding synonyms or alternative phrases that could be substituted for words used in the book.

Helen Cowcher uses the word 'grasslands' at the beginning of the story, which serves as a good, clear example of a compound word and can be used to foster an interest in how compound words are created.

THE POSTER
SIDE ONE

This side of the poster shows a simple map of Africa, which links to the non-fiction work on page 11. The map will help to give the children an idea of how large Africa is. They will probably find it of interest to be given a brief explanation as to how the countries within it are so different. Dotted around the map are pictures of the animals that share the plains with the rhinos and giraffes. These will be the focus of the research work undertaken by the mixed-ability groups.

SIDE TWO

This side of the poster is linked to the poetry activity on page 14. On one half of the poster there is a 'Giraffe Poem' that is a model for the more able group to use. On the other half is the poetry scaffold for the other groups to use and extend.

LINKED RESOURCES
OTHER BOOKS BY HELEN COWCHER

Rainforest; Antarctica; Tigress; Jaguar (all published by Scholastic Ltd.)

PICTURE BOOKS WITH ANIMAL CHARACTERS

Keeping with Cheetah Lindsay Camp and Jill Newton (Mantra)
The House Cat Helen Cooper (Picture Hippo)
Tom's Tail Linda Jennings and Tim Warnes (Magi Publications)
The Black and White Cat Deborah King (Red Fox)
Elephants Don't Do Ballet Penny McKinlay and Graham Percy (illustrator) (Frances Lincoln)
The Brave Hare Dave and Judy Saunders (Frances Lincoln)
Animal Stories Dick King Smith (Puffin)
Tigerella Kit Wright and Peter Bailey (illustrator) (Picture Hippo)

STORIES FROM AFRICA

Tales from the African Plains Anne Gatti and Gregory Alexander (illustrator) (Pavilion Classics)
Classic African Children's Stories - A Collection of Ancient Tales Phyllis Savory (editor) (Carol Publishing Group)

BOOKS ABOUT ENVIRONMENTAL ISSUES

Anthology for the Earth Judy Allen (Walker Books)
Beyond the Rainbow Warrior... Michael Morpurgo (editor) (Pavilion)
What on Earth...? Poems with a Conservation Theme Judith Nicholls (Faber and Faber)

LESSON PLANS

BEFORE READING

LET'S LOOK AT THE BOOK COVER
RESOURCES NEEDED

Big Book version of *Whistling Thorn* (optional), a selection of picture books (include some which have the same author and illustrator and others which have different authors and illustrators), board or flip chart, photocopiable page 21 (make an enlarged copy for demonstration with the whole class).

WHOLE-CLASS WORK

This activity involves looking closely at the information conveyed on the front and back cover of the book, and making predictions about the story based on this. It is important that children become familiar with using appropriate terminology to talk about the features they will find on book covers, such as *title*, *author*, *blurb*. The meanings of some or all of these may need to be explained as you work through this activity.

Show the children the cover of *Whistling Thorn* (use the Big Book if available) and begin by asking them what features they notice on both the front and the back. Use the terms *title*, *author*, *illustration*, *spine*, *blurb* (without reading it!), *publisher*, *bar code*, *price* and *ISBN*, and explain each of these as they arise in the discussion. Draw the children's attention to the fact that *Whistling Thorn* is written and illustrated by the same person, whereas many picture books are written by one person and illustrated by another. Show them examples of both types of book.

Ask the children what they understand by the word *Whistling* in the title and encourage them to put it into a context and sentence of their own, for instance 'whistling a tune' or 'the wind whistling through the trees'. Similarly, ask them what they understand about the word *thorn*. Ask if any of them have encountered this word before and where they might find a thorn. Suggestions may include on a bunch of roses or a rose bush. Now look at the front cover with the children and ask them if they can see anything that could be a thorn in the picture, thus making a link between the title and the illustration. Encourage the children to try to describe what is happening in the picture and then to make connections with the title, making deductions and predictions about the story that is to follow. On the board or flip chart, make a note of any key words that crop up. These can act as a prompt for the children or help them with spelling.

GROUP WORK

Give each child a copy of photocopiable page 21 (differentiation in this activity will be through outcome). Using your enlarged copy, demonstrate to the children what you would like them to do. Explain that using the picture of the front cover, you want them to identify and label the title, author, cover illustration and publisher's sign. In the space underneath they must make some predictions about what they think the book is going to be about. They can use the words from the list created in the whole-class session to help them.

PLENARY

Ask the children to share their versions of what they think the story is going to be about. Try to get as many different predictions as possible. Encourage the children to be sensitive and tactful when expressing their views about the likelihood of the predictions made. Draw out their reasons and and ask them to justify their opinions.

To conclude the lesson, give the children some more information about the author and the story. Tell them that Helen Cowcher is particularly interested in

LESSON PLANS

environmental issues and read them the blurb from the back of the book. Briefly ask the children if this extra information has changed their opinions of what the story might be about.

THE MAIN EVENTS
RESOURCES NEEDED

Big Book version of *Whistling Thorn* (optional), photocopiable page 22 (enlarged to A3 if possible), writing materials, board or flip chart.

WHOLE-CLASS WORK

This session will ensure that the children are familiar with the story, and will provide a good basis around which other work can be done.

Read through the story with the whole class. (Use the Big Book if available.) As you do this, draw the children's attention to elements and ideas in the book that they may not have met before:
✷ The story is set in Africa, in the wide open spaces called 'plains'.
✷ The rhinos only ate when they were hungry, but the giraffe 'grazed' all day, eating constantly.
✷ The thorns that the acacia bushes grew are like the thorns on a rose bush, and act as a means of protection.
✷ The thorns on the acacia bushes whistled because they had holes in them which made a sound when air was blown through them, just like wind instruments, such as recorders, do.

After you have read the story, ask the children what they have learned from it. Suggestions may include what rhinos and giraffes like to eat, the different eating habits between the two animals, that ants like nectar and made their nests in the thorns, that living things change in order to survive.

Ask the children to imagine that they are going to tell someone the story, but they must do so in only four sentences. Stress that because they only have four sentences, they must think very carefully about what they consider to be the most important parts of the story. Give the children some time to think about what they would like to say then collect and scribe their ideas on the board. With the class, discuss which of the sentences are the most important. Guide the children towards the points listed here to clarify the main ideas:
✷ The giraffes' constant grazing meant that the acacia bushes would soon all be eaten.
✷ The acacia bushes grew thorns and galls, which the ants were attracted to and lived in.

LITERACY HOUR UNITS   WHISTLING THORN

LESSON PLANS

* When the giraffes ate the acacia leaves, the ants came out and crawled all over their muzzles.
* The acacia bushes were protected by the ants so the giraffes were only able to eat for a short time before moving on to another bush, which gave the bushes a chance to grow.

Discuss these points with the children to ensure that they have a full understanding of the story. As you are working, you may like to make a list of key words which the children can refer to later.

GROUP WORK

Give each child a copy of photocopiable page 22. Point out the four boxes and explain that you want the children to write a sentence in each box explaining the main events of the story. Younger or less able children can draw pictures showing the different events. The children can either work individually or in groups. A display of key words from the text will help guide the children with the retelling and spelling.

PLENARY

Ask the children to share their work with the rest of the class. Discuss sensitively whether all the important elements have been covered in the individual's or group's work.

FINDING OUT MEANINGS OF WORDS FROM THE TEXT

RESOURCES NEEDED

Big Book version of *Whistling Thorn* (optional), photocopiable pages 23 and 24, dictionaries, scissors, A4 sugar paper, glue, board or flip chart, different-coloured chalks or marker pens, examples of glossaries from children's information books.

WHOLE-CLASS WORK

Much of the vocabulary in *Whistling Thorn* is very challenging for this age-group and will need to be explained in order for the children to have a full understanding of the story.

Write out the following sentences on a large piece of paper and highlight the words in italics by writing them in a different colour.

Giraffe stretched out his long tongue and *grasped* the juicy rich leaves.
Rhino, like all his *fellow* rhinos, rested for hours in the shade, each day...
But the giraffes ate *constantly*.
He *rocked* the gall homes!
Frenzied ants scrambled out, crawling in a steady stream all over the giraffe's *muzzle*, stinging as they went.

In turn, find each of these sentences in the book (use the Big Book if available) and ask the children what they think the words you have written in coloured pen might mean. Explain that they should use the context of the story to help them. Check the words in a dictionary, modelling how to use it, and read the definitions to the children. Ask them to make suggestions about words or phrases they could substitute, for example, 'get hold of' instead of 'grasped', 'disturbed' instead of 'rocked'.

LESSON PLANS

GROUP WORK

Photocopiable pages 23 and 24 are two ability-differentiated photocopiable sheets with the same format. Give each group a copy of the book, copies of the photocopiable sheet appropriate to its ability, a dictionary, scissors, glue and a piece of A4 sugar paper. The words in bold on the sheets are from the text and the words in normal text are their definitions. Explain that, in their groups, you want the children to cut out the boxes and work together to match the words with their meanings, using their combined previous knowledge, the contextual clues from the book and a dictionary. Make sure that they check their work with you before they stick down their final version onto the sugar paper.

PLENARY

Discuss the meanings of the words that the children have been working on – they may have found other information when using the dictionary or have experience of their own to share. Ask the children to use the words in sentences of their own to show that they fully understand what they mean.

You may also like to use the words from both the class and group work sessions to make a glossary for the book. Show the children the examples of glossaries that you have gathered. Explain that a glossary is a brief dictionary at the end of a book which highlights any unusual or difficult words which have been used in the text.

GIRAFFE'S POINT OF VIEW
RESOURCES NEEDED

Big Book version of *Whistling Thorn* (optional) photocopiable page 25, flip chart/large piece of sugar paper, marker pens, writing materials.

WHOLE-CLASS WORK

With the class, determine that the key animal in this story is the giraffe, because it is the giraffe who grazes and who can reach the top branches of the bushes. It is therefore most responsible for the deterioration of the acacias.

Retell the story with particular reference to the giraffes' role. Encourage in-put from the children as you are doing so in order to generate discussion. Some key 'open' questions you could ask include:
* How does the giraffe eat the leaves from the acacia bush?
* What is the giraffe thinking as he is eating the leaves?
* What does it mean by 'the giraffes ate constantly'?
* What do you think the giraffes thought of the 'whistling thorn' noise?
* Why didn't the thorns stop the giraffe eating from the acacia bushes?
* How did the giraffe feel when the ants were climbing all over his muzzle?
* What difference did the thorns and the ants make to the giraffes' eating habits?

As the discussion progresses, make a list of key words on the flip chart or large piece of paper for the children to refer to later as a prompt for ideas and to aid spelling.

GROUP WORK

Direct the most able group to write the story from the giraffe's point of view. Ask them to imagine they are the giraffe and to write in the first person. They can use the pictures in the book to help them retell it. Their work will not necessarily reflect the actual time-scales involved in the evolution of the acacia bushes, but the story does not reflect realistic time-scales.

LITERACY HOUR UNITS   WHISTLING THORN

LESSON PLANS

Ask the children in the middle-ability group to imagine they are the giraffe as well. They should also write in the first person, and explain how feeding from the acacia bushes before and after they have thorns is different.

Give the less able groups a copy of photocopiable sheet 25 and explain that you want them to fill in the speech bubble. How do they think the giraffe feels when it tries to feed from the bush and a swarm of ants crawl all over its muzzle? Explain that they should write in the first person, using 'I' – imagining that they are the giraffe.

PLENARY

With the class, discuss the ways in which life changed for the giraffes after the acacia bushes grew galls. Ask various children from each of the groups to read out some of their work to show how well they have imagined what it would be like to be the giraffe.

ADJECTIVES
RESOURCES NEEDED

Big Book version of *Whistling Thorn* (optional), board or flip chart, dictionaries and thesauruses, A4 paper, writing materials.

WHOLE-CLASS WORK

Introduce, or recap, with the class what an adjective is. Explain that it is a describing word: it tells us what something is like. Give the children some examples such as 'a ginger cat', 'a naughty monkey', 'a comfortable chair'. You may like to use the five senses to describe an object in a concrete way, for example, 'I can see a black dog', 'I can hear a loud noise'.

Tell the children that you are going to read through the book (use the Big Book if available) and, with their help, you are going to make a list of the adjectives that the author uses. Make sure when you have done this that your list includes: *long, juicy, rich, tiniest, hungry, highest, sweet, thorny, steady, free, fresh* and *hot*.

Look at the words on the list and discuss what they mean and whether they can be used in different contexts – 'rich', for example, can be used in 'A rich person is someone who has a lot of money' or 'The cake was so rich that I could only eat a little piece'. At this stage you may also wish to introduce comparative adjectives, looking at the words 'tiniest' and 'highest'.

WHISTLING THORN | LITERACY HOUR UNITS

LESSON PLANS

GROUP WORK

Tell the children in the most able group that you would like them to find the following adjectives in the book: *juicy, tiniest, hungry, highest, sweet* and *hot*. Explain that when they have done this, you want them to write out the sentences in which these adjectives appear, but instead of using the adjectives the author has given they must substitute an alternative adjective which has the same meaning. You may like to explain at this point that a word that means the same or very nearly the same is called a synonym. Hand out the dictionaries and thesauruses for them to use.

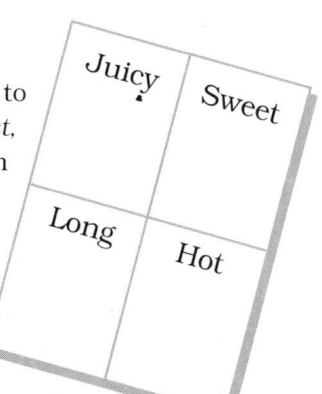

Explain to the middle ability group that you would like them to choose six adjectives from the list you made in the whole-class session, and then write them in a sentence of their own to show that they understand the meanings.

For the less able group, divide an A4 piece of paper into four sections with an adjective from the story in each box – *juicy, sweet, long* and *hot*, for example. Explain that their task is to draw in the boxes objects that these adjectives could describe. For instance in the box for 'Juicy', they could draw oranges, a melon and strawberries.

PLENARY

Start by reinforcing the definition of an adjective to ensure that the children understand what it means. Ask children from each group to discuss the work they have been doing and to give some examples. Point out that using adjectives in written work can make it much more interesting and lively to read.

READING AND WRITING NON-FICTION
RESOURCES NEEDED

Big Book version of *Whistling Thorn* (optional), a globe and/or simple map of the world, the map of Africa from the poster, a selection of information books about animals from the African plains, pencils, felt-tipped pens, glue, scissors, lined or plain paper, sheets of sugar paper, board or flip chart.

WHOLE-CLASS WORK

Whistling Thorn is essentially a 'non-fiction story'; it explains the evolution of the acacia bushes in a way that is accessible and uncomplicated for children. It therefore lends itself well to being a springboard for non-fiction work. Many of the children may have seen giraffes and other African animals in zoos or safari parks, but the book provides a lead-in to learn more about their natural habitat.

Using a globe or a simple world map, show the class where Africa is in relation to the UK. Next, refer to the map of Africa on the poster and ask the children if they have ever been to any part of Africa. Explain that it is a very large continent with varying landscapes. Point out the desert, rainforest and savannah areas and ask the children to tell you anything they know about these types of areas.

Ask the children what other animals, apart from the giraffe and rhinoceros, live in the savannah areas. On the board make a list of the animals the children suggest – lions, zebras, elephants, wildebeest.

Explain or revise what a verb is and give the class some examples. Explain that *Whistling Thorn* is written in the past tense – it tells the reader about something that has already happened and the verbs indicate this. Point out some examples of past tense verbs in the story (use the Big Book if available) and explain that many of them end in 'ed', such as *stretched, grasped* and *nibbled*. List these on the board or flip chart and ask the children to find other words from the book

LESSON PLANS

that end with 'ed'. Write these up on the board as the children suggest them, underlining the 'ed' part to draw attention to it. The words should include: *stretched, grasped, nibbled, rested, wandered, passed, shaped, smelled, piped, rocked, climbed, moved, awaited, spurred, washed, flowed.* To reinforce the difference between the present and past tense, use the list of words above in sentences using 'Yesterday' (Yesterday she climbed a ladder) and 'Today' (Today she climbs a ladder).

GROUP WORK

Organize the class into mixed-ability groups and explain that each group is going to become an expert on one of the animals of the African plains. Allow each group to choose a particular animal to study, or assign one to them. Discuss with the children what information they would like to find out about their animal. Encourage them to set their own questions but some starter questions could include:

* What does the animal look like?
* What does it eat?
* Does it have a 'home'?
* Does it live on its own or with a herd or pack?

Give each group some information books about their animal, some lined and plain paper, pencils, felt-tipped pens (optional), glue, scissors and a large piece of sugar paper on which they can present their work. Stress that when they have found the information they are looking for they must write it in their own words, not just copy it out. Refer back to the work on tenses above and explain that the writing they will be doing now is non-fiction. Therefore, they should write in the present tense because it is information that will remain constant. (You may wish to give a short explanation to the children before they start their work, highlighting some of the differences between fiction and non-fiction books. For example, the difference in tenses and style of writing that is used, the use of contents and index pages, and so on.) Explain that they will also need to draw some illustrations to accompany their information.

Leave the children to establish their own roles within the group and to decide what they are going to draw or find out, but check to see that all the children are contributing something. At intervals warn the groups how much time they have left so that they are aware of their time-limit.

PLENARY

Ask each group to give a presentation on their animal and to explain where and how they found their information. For example did they look in the index, at the contents page or did they just skim through the book? Display the children's work alongside the information books that they used.

LESSON PLANS

READING COMPREHENSION

RESOURCES NEEDED

Big Book version of *Whistling Thorn* (optional), scissors, glue, sugar paper, writing materials, photocopiable pages 26, 27 and 28.

WHOLE-CLASS WORK

When using a book with the whole class, it is essential that all the children are engaged at an appropriate level. Think carefully about the questions you ask to ensure that they extend and enrich the text.

To assess the children's basic understanding of *Whistling Thorn* while you are reading it, ask questions such as:
* Where did the acacia bushes grow?
* What is the savannah like?
* How is the giraffe's way of feeding different from the rhino's?
* Why did the thorns whistle?
* Why were the ants attracted to the galls?

However, to improve thinking skills, ask questions that involve the children bringing their own experience to the text, considering various points of view, speculating on what could have happened if part of the story had been different and making judgements about the characters and the story as a whole. For example:
* Can you think of any other animals that 'graze' like the giraffe?
* What other plants have thorns?
* How do you think the giraffe felt about the acacia bushes' thorns?
* What would have happened if the acacia bush had not grown thorns?
* Do you think it was wrong for the giraffe to eat the acacia bushes all the time?

At Key Stage One, in particular, it is important that children have opportunities to respond to texts orally as well as in written form so that they can demonstrate what they understand of the book and its wider implications. It also creates assessment opportunities.

GROUP WORK

Photocopiable page 26 poses a number of questions that are aimed to extend the more able group. Allow children to discuss the questions together so that they can share their ideas and opinions.

Photocopiable page 27 is a cloze procedure. However, it allows for some amount of open-endedness in that the children can choose words which they feel are appropriate rather than making a selection from a given bank of words. Stress to this group that there is no 'right' answer; there may be a range of words that they need to consider before writing in a suitable choice. This not only tests the children's comprehension skills, but also allows them to be creative within the structure.

Photocopiable page 28 is for the less able group, but they may still need support with reading it. Explain to the group that the three columns contain the beginnings, middles and ends of sentences. The children's job is to cut out the boxes in each column and match them up correctly. They must first check with an adult that they have placed the sentences in the right order before sticking them onto a piece of sugar paper. This activity will be an indication as to whether or not the children have a basic understanding of the story.

LESSON PLANS

PLENARY

Ask children from each group to feed back examples of their work. Stress the fact that individuals interpret things differently and have varying ideas. Discuss some of the answers written for the questions and cloze procedure (photocopiable pages 26 and 27). Ask the children which ones they think fitted best. Remind them that they must support their opinions with reasons.

GIRAFFE POEMS

RESOURCES NEEDED

Big Book version of *Whistling Thorn* (optional), board or flip chart, the 'Giraffe poem' and poetry scaffold side of the poster, writing materials.

WHOLE-CLASS WORK

Whistling Thorn gives the reader some incidental information about the giraffe, and the illustrations are detailed and accurate. Using the pictures as a basis, brainstorm with the children what they know about giraffes – what they look like, where they live, what they eat, how they eat, and so on. Scribe the children's comments on the board or flip chart for them to use as a prompt and refer back to later – they will have a bank of ideas and spellings on which to draw. Ideas you could include are: *tall, long-legged, spotty, speckly, spindly, long-lashed, hooves, big eyes, chewing, grazing* and *nibbling*.

GROUP WORK

Ask the more able group to make up an eight line poem of their own. They can use the ideas they brainstormed in the class session and the model of the Giraffe poem from the poster.

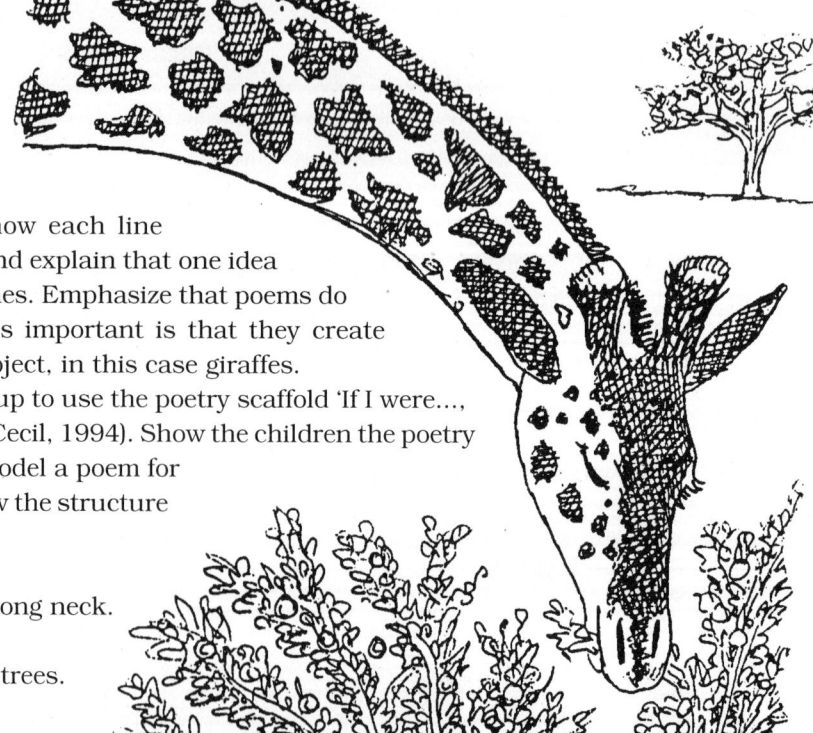

The giraffe is standing
Proud and tall,
Looking over the plains
And seeing all.
He is nibbling leaves,
He never stops,
Bending his long neck
Over acacia tree tops.

Point out to the children how each line begins with a capital letter and explain that one idea can be developed over two lines. Emphasize that poems do not have to rhyme – what is important is that they create interesting images of the subject, in this case giraffes.

Tell the middle-ability group to use the poetry scaffold 'If I were…, I would/could…' (Nancy Lee Cecil, 1994). Show the children the poetry scaffold on the poster and model a poem for them so that they can see how the structure will work, for example:

If I were a giraffe,
I would have a long, strong neck.
If I were a giraffe,
I could see over tops of trees.
If I were a giraffe,
I would graze all day long.
If I were a giraffe,
I would look down on the world.

LESSON PLANS

Less able children can also use the poetry scaffold, but allow them to work in pairs or to write a group poem with the aid of an adult. The number of lines in the scaffolded poem can vary according to the children's ability and enthusiasm.

Tell the children in all the groups to copy up their poems. These can then be made into a display or a book of 'Giraffe Poems'.

PLENARY

Select children from each group to share their poems with the class. Ask them to talk about what they have learned about poetry and to discuss the process of writing and editing. *What changes did you make, if any? Are you happy with the final version? Would you do anything differently next time you wrote a poem?*

RETELLING THE STORY

RESOURCES NEEDED

Big Book version of *Whistling Thorn* (optional), large piece of paper, marker pen, paper, pencils, card, coloured pencils or pens, glue or sellotape, lollipop sticks/ magnetic board and magnets/velcro board and velcro pieces to make puppets or figures, some examples of children's plays.

WHOLE-CLASS WORK

Retelling the story in their own words will give children ownership of the story and consolidate and assess their understanding of the book.

Cover up the text and ask the children to retell the story from the pictures. Encourage them to elaborate on what they see, and to extend and embellish the story, adding some traditional story language such as, 'Long, long ago on the plains of Africa...' or 'When the cruel winds swept across the savannah...'. Prompt them by asking what the giraffe might be feeling at different points in the story, and so on. The children may find it helpful if you retell the story before they attempt to do so as this will act as a model for them to use in their own storytelling.

GROUP WORK

Ensure that the children are familiar with the story. Allow all the groups some time to look through the books to establish the characters. Explain that you will be asking the groups to make models of the characters in the books so the children must make a mental note of any props they feel they will need to use.

Ask the more able children to work together in small groups and to write a simple playscript that they can act out. (This group will require more focused attention from the teacher or a helper.) Work through some plays with them first so that they become familiar with the format. Talk about the role of the narrator, the need for 'stage directions' and how direct speech is set out with the characters' names. You may wish to write a few lines to start them off. For example:

The giraffe and the rhino were feeding from the acacia bush.
    Rhino: I've had enough of these juicy acacia leaves. I'm going to rest in
    th shade.
    Giraffe: Well, I could eat all day – in fact, I probably will!
The rhino moves off and the giraffe continues to graze.

Ask the other groups to act out the story using either stick puppets or a storyboard background with magnetic or velcro figures. Stick puppets can be

LESSON PLANS

made simply by drawing figures on to paper. These can then be cut out, coloured in, glued to pieces of thin card and attached to sticks which can then be moved around. The children will also need to think about the back-drop and other props that they will need. The figures can be moved in and out of a scene as they appear.

Encourage all the children to contribute when discussing the process and performing. Stress the notion that storytelling is not static. It is an everchanging process and will, in fact, change every time the story is retold. Their version does not have to be an exact replica of the story told in the book. Encourage them to embellish the story and to be confident in giving it their own interpretation.

PLENARY

Before the children show their 'performances' to one another, ask them to reflect on the processes they went through when creating their production. Pose some key questions such as: *How did you decide what roles to take on? How did you decide on your starting point for the story? Which bits of the story, if any, did you think needed to be expanded? Which parts were vital to include to understand the story? What is the role of the narrator? What did you learn about how playscripts work? How are they different from storybooks? What must you remember when writing a playscript?*

USING CONJUNCTIONS
RESOURCES NEEDED

Big Book version of *Whistling Thorn* (optional) flip chart or large sheet of paper, small pieces of paper or thin card, photocopiable pages 29 and 30.

WHOLE-CLASS WORK

Talk to the children about how two shorter sentences can be joined together with the conjunction *and*. Read out some examples from the book that the author uses, inserting a pronoun where necessary:

✱ Giraffe stretched out his long tongue and [he] grasped the juicy rich leaves.
✱ Rhino, like all his fellow rhinos, rested for hours in the shade each day and [he] only wandered to the acacias when he felt very hungry.
✱ The wind came blowing across the savannah and [it] piped through the holes like the music of a thousand flutes.

Ask the children to think of other words that could be substituted for the word 'and' in each of the sentences above. In the first sentence, they might suggest *while* or *then*, for the second they may suggest *then* or *so* and for the third *but* or *as*.

On a large sheet of paper or the flip chart, begin compiling a list of conjunctions that can join two short sentences together and encourage the children to make contributions. The first words on the list should be simple ones that the children are familiar with reading and writing, for example *and, but, then, so*. Keep the list up in the classroom so that the children can add to it as they think of or come across more conjunction words. They can move on to phrases when they become more familiar with the idea, for example, *and after that, then later on*.

As many of the sentences from the book are quite complicated, the children may find it helpful if you show them other examples of short sentences that are linked by simple conjunctions. Explain that in a sentence various conjunctions may all be appropriate. For example:

We went outside _____ the sun was shining. (because, and, although, when...)

LESSON PLANS

The sun was shining _____ we went outside. (so, when, after, before...)

Give the children opportunities to offer their own suggestions for filling in the gaps in the examples. Then ask them to make up some sentences of their own that can be linked by conjunctions. Give out the pieces of paper or thin card and tell them to write their conjunctions on these. The children can then try them in their various sentences to see whether they 'fit'.

GROUP WORK

When the children are confident with using conjunctions, and are able to pick them out in sentences, give them the photocopiable sheets to work on. Both sheets use ideas and vocabulary from the story.

Photocopiable page 29 is for the more able group and requires the children to choose their own conjunctions to fit into the spaces in the sentences, and then to make up some sentences of their own using conjunctions. Asking the children to make up some sentences of their own will enable you to see how well they have understood the activity.

Photocopiable page 30 is for less able children. They must choose an appropriate word from the conjunctions offered on the sheet and then make up some sentences of their own using conjunctions. This group may need support with reading the sentences on the sheet. Alternatively, the photocopiable sheet can be enlarged and worked through as a group activity, with support from an adult helper.

PLENARY

Ask the children to report back which conjunctions they used to complete the photocopiable sheets. Stress that differing words will still 'fit'. Allow children to share some of their own sentences too, as this will help to increase their confidence. Explain that to make a text lively and interesting for the reader it is important to use a variety of vocabulary and conjunctions in their work.

COMPOUND WORDS
RESOURCES NEEDED

Big Book version of *Whistling Thorn* (optional), a board or flip chart, photocopiable page 31, dictionaries, scissors, paper, glue, writing materials.

WHOLE-CLASS WORK

Pick out the word 'grasslands' from the text (use the Big Book if available) and ask the children what they think it means. Hopefully, they will give you the answer 'land covered in grass'. Explain that this is called a compound word: it consists of two words that have been joined together to make another word. Give the class some more examples, such as *cupcake, mousetrap, stairway* and *armchair* and write these on the board or flip chart. To illustrate the point, draw a thin line between the two words that make up the compound words. Write up the word 'sun' and ask the children if they can think of any words that could be added to 'sun' to make compound words. Suggestions may include *shine, day, shade, bed, set, beam*. Write these up also.

Hopefully, by now the children will be becoming familiar with the idea of compound words and may be able to offer some of their own examples. If they need

LESSON PLANS

further practice, offer them a few more 'halves' of words to finish, for example 'wind' could become windmill, windsurfer or windscreen; 'rain' could become raincoat, rainbow or raindrop.

Use these words to start a class list of compound words. Write them up on a large sheet of paper and leave this in the classroom for the children to add to as they think of further words.

GROUP WORK

On a sheet of paper write these words out for the more able group – *water*, *tea*, *under*, *over*, *ice*, *land*. Explain that their task is to think of compound words using these words. Allow the group time to come up with their own ideas and discuss possibilities. Give the children dictionaries so that they can check their work and look for other compound words that they have not thought about.

Give the children in the other group a copy of photocopiable page 31. Explain that they must cut out the boxes in both columns and then match the words so that they create compound words. (The words in bold will always come first.) Have dictionaries available for them to check their work. When they have checked their words, ask them to stick their pairs of words onto a sheet of paper. The third column contains empty boxes. Explain that after the children have completed the first part of the activity they can use these boxes to create other compound words.

PLENARY

Ask the groups to report back on the compound words they have made. Did any of words they wrote turn out not to be compound words? Did the first group find some of the words more challenging than others? Did the dictionaries provide many words to add to their lists and did they understand all of these words? Did the children who did the 'matching' activity find that more than one word matched the word in italics? Give the children opportunites to add their words to the class list, if they are not there already.

STORY WRITING
RESOURCES NEEDED

A flip chart/large sheet of paper and a marker pen, photocopiable page 32, plus an enlarged copy for demonstration with the class, writing materials.

WHOLE-CLASS WORK

When the class know the story of *Whistling Thorn* well, they can use it to model a story of their own. Explain that in this lesson you want the children to write a story on 'How the rose got its thorn'. Begin by asking who or what might be a threat to the survival of the rose bush. Discuss the attractions of the rose – sweet-smelling, beautiful to look at, and so on. Make a note of the children's suggestions on a flip chart or large piece of paper so that they can refer to it later. Discuss the idea that in order to protect itself the rose bush, over a period of time, grew sharp thorns to deter people or animals from gathering or disturbing them. Ask the children to describe a scene in which a person or animal tries to pick a rose which has newly acquired thorns. Make a note of the key words.

Explain to the children that you are going to show them how to plan a story of their own. Remind them that stories have beginnings, middles and ends. Look at

LESSON PLANS

the first page of *Whistling Thorn* - the story begins 'Long ago, on the grasslands of Africa, there grew acacia bushes.' Explain that the book is setting the scene for the whole story and ask them for other story beginnings, such as 'Once upon a time...' or 'In a place not far from here...'. Point out that in the introduction, they need to include the time, place and main characters.

Move on to discussing the middle part of the story. The middle section will begin by outlining a problem or conflict to be resolved. The roles of the characters also need to be established – how they fit into the overall plot, whether they are 'good' or 'bad'. This is the bulk of the story and will include the 'action' leading to a resolution. In *Whistling Thorn* for example, the problem is that the acacia bushes are being wiped out, mainly by the giraffes. The ants play their role by inhabiting the thorn galls and defending their homes by crawling over the giraffes' muzzles, thus solving the danger of the demise of the bushes.

Read the last page of *Whistling Thorn* to the children and point out how the story is concluded – the animals are content because they can still eat the acacia leaves, but the ants allow the bushes time to grow. The scene described is peaceful and has a sense of well-being. It is a happy ending to the story. Encourage the children to try to get a similar feeling at the end of their stories.

Show the children the story planner on photocopiable page 32. Explain that there are words to help them listed down the sides, but these are suggestions and the children do not have to use them in their stories. Emphasize that this is the planning stage. They should use this time to try out ideas. They can also write down ideas in note form rather than sentences – they can expand their writing and ideas when they write out their story later.

GROUP WORK

The more able groups can use the story planner individually or in pairs. When they have finished their planner and are happy with their ideas, they should copy up their story.

An adult helper will be required to work with the less able group on a collaborative story. Using your enlarged version of the photocopiable sheet ask the children for their ideas about the story. Discuss and agree each point before writing it up on the planner. When the group has finished, the children can use the planner to help them write and draw a 'cartoon' version of the story.

PLENARY

Ask the children about the process of writing their stories. Which part did they find most difficult to write? Did they use the ideas they discussed in the class group or did they think of their own? What vocabulary have they used to describe the rose, or what happened when someone tried to pick it? Ask the children to share their stories with the whole class or within their group.

LITERACY HOUR UNITS   WHISTLING THORN

LESSON PLANS

BOOK REVIEW

RESOURCES NEEDED

Large sheets of paper/flip chart, marker pens, photocopiable page 22 (when photocopying this page, you will need to blank out the grid in the middle of the page so that only the border is retained), writing materials, coloured pencils.

WHOLE-CLASS WORK

In order to become critical readers, children need to form and express opinions about the books they read. Oral or written reviews are a good way of focusing children on the text and encouraging them to think beyond books just being 'funny' or 'boring'.

Begin by asking them to summarize what the book was about. They should be able to say that the story tells of how the acacia bush protected itself by changing so that it could survive the giraffes feeding from it constantly. Write some key words from the children's summaries on a large piece of paper so that they can refer to this later for prompts and spelling. Ask which parts of the story they enjoyed most, but tell them that they must qualify their choice with reasons, 'I liked the part where... because...'. Any children who did not enjoy the book must also give their reasons why they did not like it. Encourage the children to describe what they have learned from the book, for instance that plants change and evolve to protect themselves, that giraffes eat constantly, what the African plains are like, and so on.

GROUP WORK

Each group's activity is to write a review of some kind of *Whistling Thorn* on the photocopiable border page (it may be necessary to make a draft copy first).

Ask the more able group to write a brief summary of the story (two or three sentences), explaining what they liked or disliked about it. They must give reasons, state what they have learned from the book and draw a scene from the story. Write prompts on a large piece of paper or flip chart to keep the group focused.

The middle group's task is more structured. Ask them to answer direct questions about the book. *Did you enjoy the book? Why/why not? What was your favourite part of the book? What did you learn from the book?* Write these on a large piece of paper in a prominent place so that the children can refer to them. When they have answered the questions they should draw a scene from the story.

Ask the less able children to draw their favourite scene from the book and to write why they liked it.

The children's work can be used for a display or made into a 'Book of Reviews' for the book corner.

PLENARY

Ask children from each group to share their work with the rest of the class. Pick out any common points that arise and emphasize these. For instance, many children may have said that they enjoyed the part where the ants crawled over the giraffe's muzzle so that he had to stop eating the acacia leaves, or that they learned that giraffes 'graze' or eat constantly. Be positive about the children's comments so that they build up confidence to talk and write about other books.

PHOTOCOPIABLE

Name _____   Date _____

PREDICTING THE STORY FROM THE COVER

✱ In the labels write down which parts of this cover show the **title**, **the author**, **the cover illustration** and **the publisher's sign**.

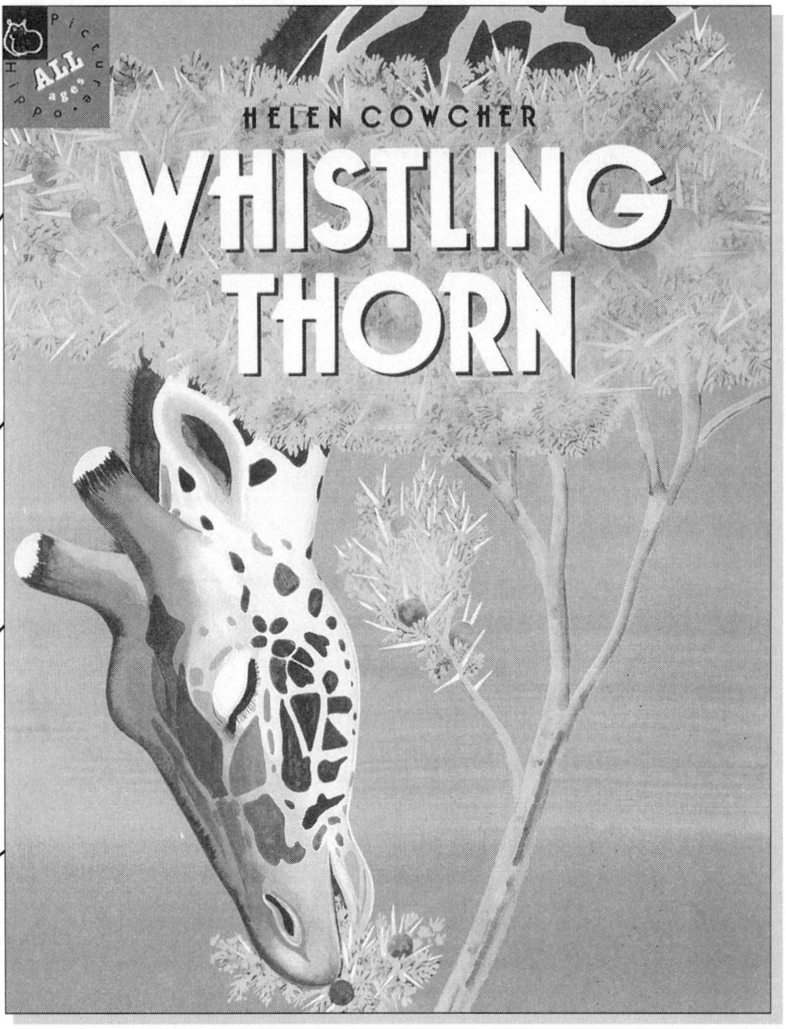

Now, using the information on the front cover, write down what you think the book is going to be about.

_____
_____
_____
_____
_____

LITERACY HOUR UNITS   21   WHISTLING THORN

Name _____  Date _____

THE FOUR MAIN EVENTS OF THE STORY

WHISTLING THORN — LITERACY HOUR UNITS

MATCHING WORDS AND MEANINGS (1)

Can you work out what these words mean?
* Cut out the boxes and match the words to their meanings.

WORDS	MEANINGS
savannah	made your way over rough ground
relentlessly	future
frenzied	hurt or damage
contentedly	went from place to place without a purpose
fate	excited
scrambled	without stopping, or all the time
harm	peacefully
wandered	a grassy open space with few trees

LITERACY HOUR UNITS — WHISTLING THORN

Name _____   Date _____

MATCHING WORDS AND MEANINGS (2)

Can you work out what these words mean?
✸ Cut out the boxes and match the words to their meanings.

WORDS	MEANINGS
bush	a stiff point on a plant
nibbled	was still or asleep
rested	a shrub, like a small tree
entrance	moving with the body close to the ground
thorn	ate in small amounts, taking little bites
crawling	way in

WHISTLING THORN   LITERACY HOUR UNITS

| Name | Date |

WHAT IS THE GIRAFFE SAYING?

What do you think the giraffe might say when the ants crawl all over his muzzle?
* Write it in the speech bubble.

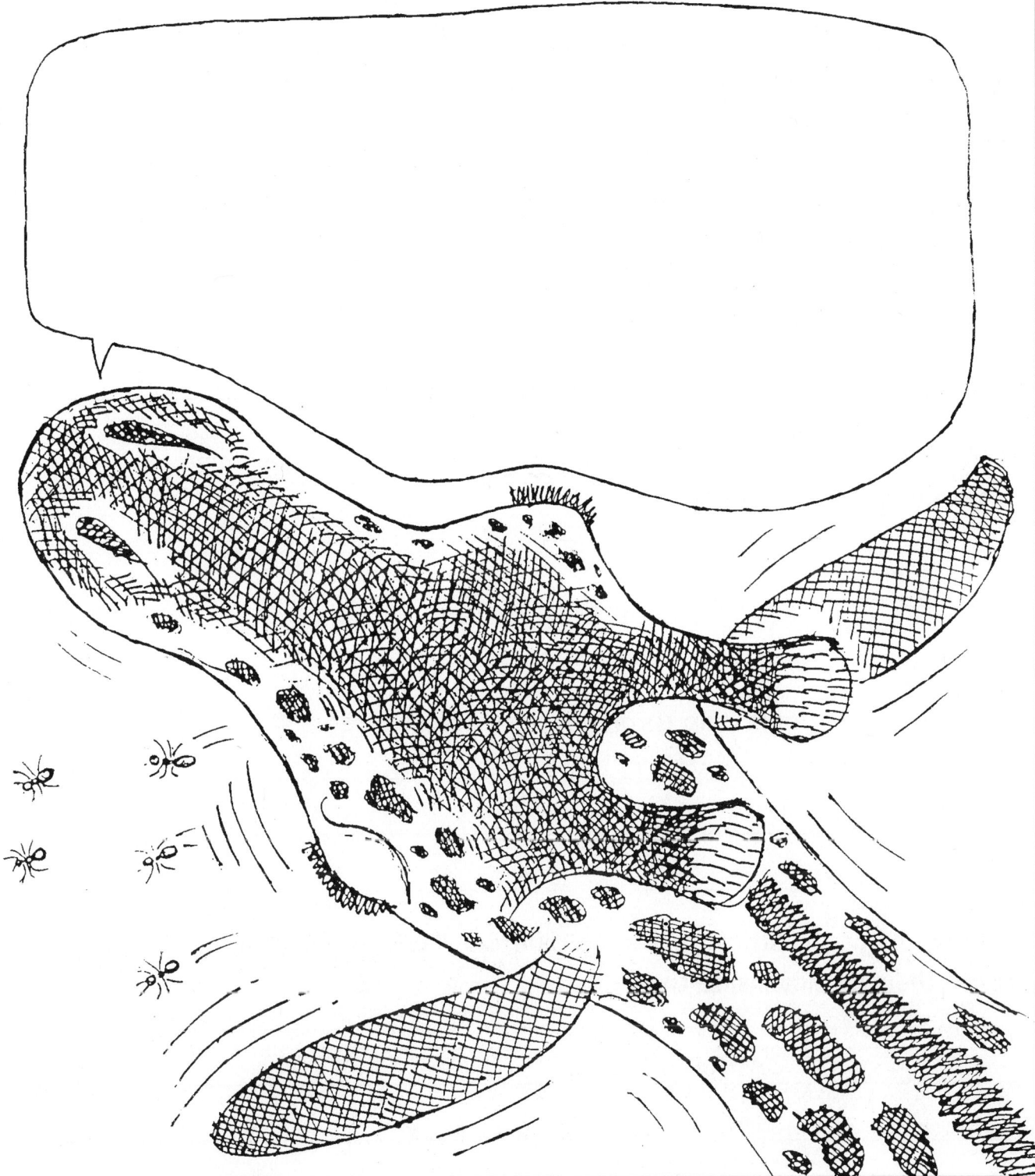

LITERACY HOUR UNITS — WHISTLING THORN

COMPREHENSION (1)

✸ Think carefully about your answers, then write them in the spaces.

1. Giraffes and rhinos are herbivores, which means they only eat plants, not meat. Why do you think this is?

___

2. Can you think of other plants that protect themselves in some way from being eaten or picked?

___

3. Why do you think the author has used colours such as orange, pink, and purple in the pictures?

___

4. How could people help to protect the acacia tree?

___

5. How might the story have been different if the ants had not made their homes inside the galls?

___

COMPREHENSION (2)

✹ Fill in the spaces with words that will 'fit' the sentences. Think carefully about the words you use.

The African savannah is _____ and _____.

The giraffes and rhinos _____ to eat the acacia _____.

The rhino ate and then _____, but the giraffe _____ all the time. The acacia trees grew _____ thorns to _____ themselves. Ants made _____ in the thorns because they were attracted by the _____ smell. The holes in the thorns made them _____ when the _____ blew. When the _____ tried to eat the thorns, the ants _____ over them. This stopped the giraffes from _____ all the acacia trees so that they are still around _____.

LITERACY HOUR UNITS   WHISTLING THORN

PHOTOCOPIABLE

Name _____   Date _____

COMPREHENSION (3)

✻ Cut out the boxes. Then match them up to create sentences. (You should have three boxes in each sentence.)

The rhinos	made their nests in the galls	because they smelled sweet.
The acacia trees	stopped eating so many acacia leaves	that looked like galls.
The ants	whistled like flutes	because the ants stung them.
The thorns	grew sharp thorns	and then rested in the shade.
The giraffes	ate the acacia leaves	when the wind blew.

Name _____ Date _____

CONJUNCTIONS (1)

✸ Fill in these sentences with a conjunction. Don't use 'and'!

1. The rhinos and giraffes lived on the grasslands _____ they liked to eat acacia leaves.

2. Giraffe ate all the time _____ Rhino ate when he was hungry.

3. Rhino went to the shade _____ he rested for hours.

4. Rhino didn't eat as much as Giraffe _____ he didn't do so much harm.

5. The acacias grew sharp thorns _____ they needed to protect themselves.

6. It sounded like a thousand flutes _____ the wind blew through the holes in the galls.

7. Giraffe tugged hard at the bushes _____ he wanted to eat the acacia leaves.

8. The ants came out of the galls _____ the giraffe rocked their homes.

9. The ants crawled over his muzzle _____ the giraffe shook his head.

10. The acacia trees survived _____ the ants protected them.

✸ Now write some sentences of your own using conjunctions.

LITERACY HOUR UNITS — WHISTLING THORN

CONJUNCTIONS 2

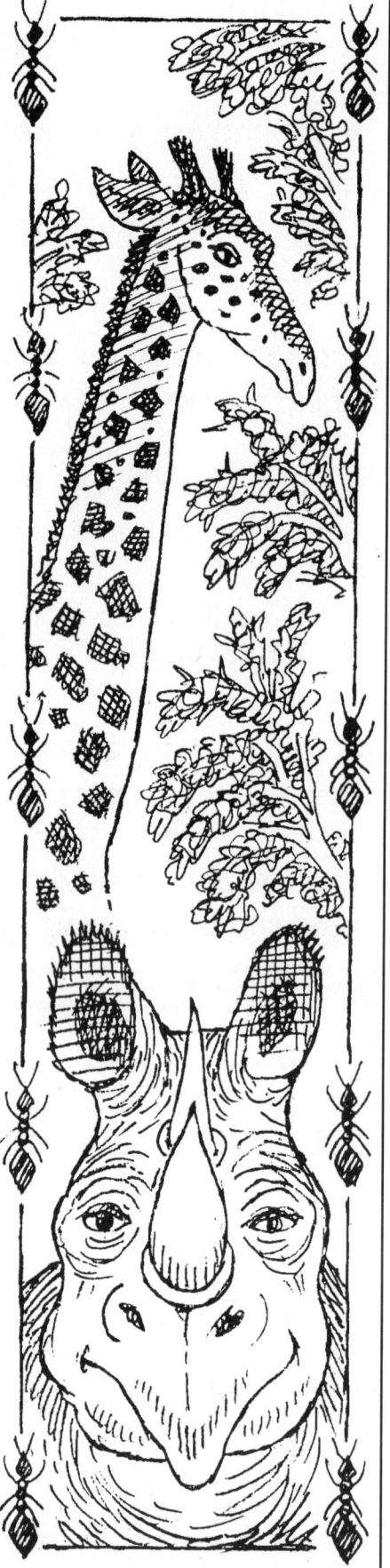

✱ Fill in the sentences using these conjunctions.

> but when so because when if so because

Giraffes like acacia leaves _____
they are juicy.

Rhinos eat when they are hungry
_____ giraffes eat all the time.

The rhinos were tired _____
they rested in the shade.

The acacia trees grew thorns
_____ they needed to
protect themselves.

The ants came to make their nests
_____ they smelled the
sweet nectar.

The thorns were sharp _____
you touched them.

The thorns whistled _____
the wind blew across the savannah.

The giraffe rocked the gall homes
_____ the ants crawled out.

✱ Now write five more sentences using
conjunctions. You can use the back of this sheet.

PHOTOCOPIABLE

Name _____   Date _____

COMPOUND WORDS

✷ Cut out the boxes. Then match up the words to make compound words. In the empty boxes create some other compound words.

tea	mark	
sun	way	
book	box	
pea	house	
rail	pot	
green	ship	
flag	flower	
paint	nut	

LITERACY HOUR UNITS — WHISTLING THORN

PHOTOCOPIABLE

Name _____   Date _____

HOW THE ROSE GOT ITS THORN

✸ Use this sheet to help you plan your story. Use the words around the boxes if you need some ideas.

long ago...	**Beginning**	once upon a time...
garden		bush
Summer		fragrant
beautiful		delicate
pretty		petal
gather	**Middle**	pick
protect		threat
survive		grew
prickly		pricked
hurt	**End**	'Ouch!'
blood		dropped
grow		leave
peace		enjoy
stay		happy

WHISTLING THORN   LITERACY HOUR UNITS